Rainy Day Activities
for Preschool Teachers

Jean Feldman

Jean Feldman

rainy day activities

Jean Feldman

Illustrations by K. Whelan Dery

gryphon house
Beltsville, MD

Acknowledgments

Special thanks to Kathy Charner, who is the best editor and magician of all! She can take my ideas and scribbles and turn them into a wonderful book for teachers.

Thanks to all the teachers who so generously shared their ideas and "tricks" with me so that I could pass them on to you.

Thanks to the children whose smiles, laughter, and twinkling eyes continue to verify that the activities in this book do work.

And thanks to my family who humors me, supports me, and is, indeed, the wind beneath my wings!

Gryphon House books are available at special discount when purchased in bulk for special premiums and sales promotions as well as for fundraising use. Special editions or book excerpts also can be created to specification. For details, contact the Director of Marketing at Gryphon House.

Copyright © 2000, Jean Feldman.
Published by Gryphon House, Inc. 10726 Tucker Street, Beltsville MD 207025. P.O. Box 207, Beltsville MD 20705-0207, USA.

Cover Illustration and Interior Illustrations by K. Whelan Dery.

Requests for permission to make copies of any part of the work should be mailed to Gryphon House, Inc.

Library of Congress Cataloging-in-Publication Data
Feldman, Jean R., 1947–
  Rainy day activities for preschool teachers / Jean Feldman; illustrations by K. Whelan Dery.
     p. cm.
  Includes index.
  ISBN 0-87659-212-4
     1. Education, Preschool—Activity programs. I. Title.

LB1140.35.C74 F45 2000
372.13—dc21

00-035366

Table of Contents

Get Up and Get Moving!

Paddle Ball

When?

It's a rainy day and you're out of ideas! Try this simple game to release energy and develop eye-hand coordination.

What?   **How?**

paper plates

crayons

scissors

stapler

scrap paper

masking tape

- Let each child decorate two paper plates with crayons.
- Cut a small curve out of one plate as shown, then staple the two plates together.
- Wad up a piece of scrap paper and wrap masking tape around it to make a ball.
- Children insert their hand in the paper plate and use it like a bat to hit the ball.
- After children have practiced, they may try to volley the ball back and forth with a friend.

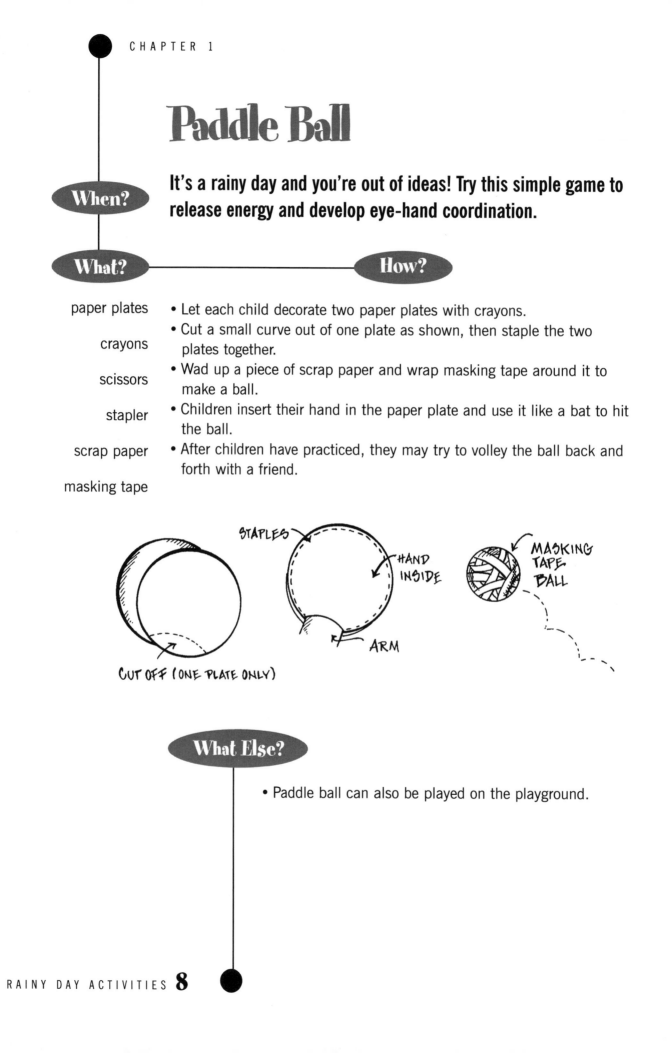

CUT OFF (ONE PLATE ONLY)

STAPLES

HAND INSIDE

ARM

MASKING TAPE BALL

What Else?

- Paddle ball can also be played on the playground.

Space Ball

Children release energy and practice eye-hand coordination with this recycled ball.

- Cut off one leg of the pantyhose from the knee down.
- Take the remaining leg and panty section and stuff it down into the toe of the leg you cut off.
- Tie a knot around the ball you have made in the toe.
- Toss the ball across the room and watch it sail like something in space.
- Let the children toss it up and try to catch it individually, or toss it to a friend.
- Place a box or basket in the center of the room, and encourage the children to try to toss their space balls in the box.

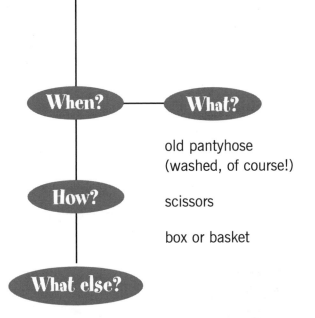

When?

What?

old pantyhose (washed, of course!)

How?

scissors

box or basket

What else?

- Have children bring in old pantyhose from home and make their own space balls. Let them decorate them with markers and fringe the tails.
- Ask children to create their own games to play with their space balls.

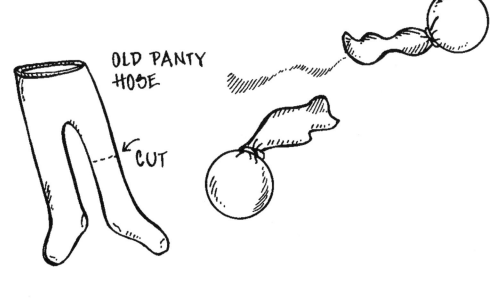

OLD PANTY HOSE

CUT

Catch and Review

When?

Use an old beach ball with this lively way to reinforce coordination and concepts.

What?

How?

beach ball, playground ball, or other large ball

permanent marker

• Sit in a circle on the floor and play one (or more) of the following games:

Rhyme Ball–Say a word, then gently throw the ball to a child. The child says a word that rhymes, then rolls the ball back to the teacher.

Letter Ball–Write letters on the ball with a permanent marker. When the teacher gently throws the ball to a child, he must identify the letter on top or think of a word that begins with that sound before rolling the ball to another friend.

Numeral Ball–Write numerals on the ball, then have children identify the numeral on top as they catch the ball.

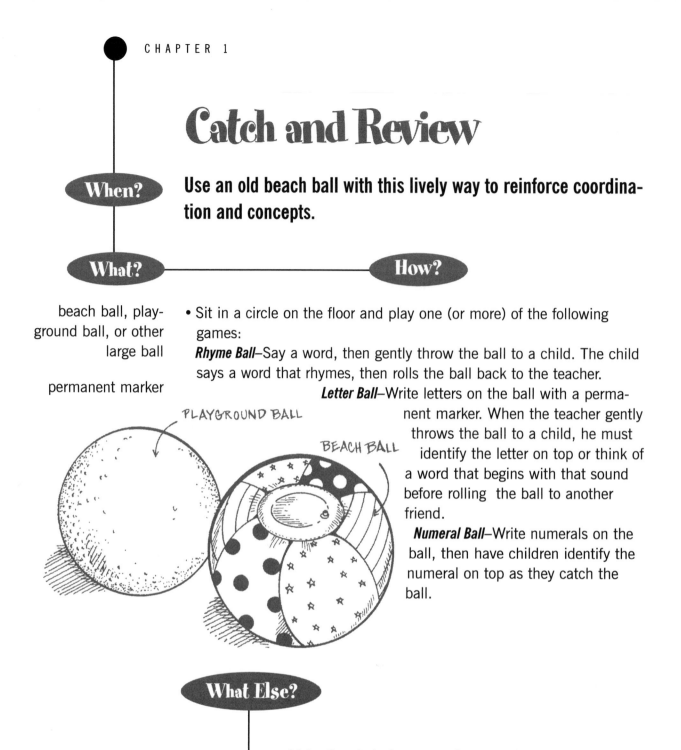

PLAYGROUND BALL

BEACH BALL

What Else?

• Make the circle larger, so the game is more challenging.
• Try catching the ball after one or two bounces.

Can Catch

This simple toy made from recycled materials is sure to please the children.

- Demonstrate how to bounce the tennis ball, then catch it in the can.
- Challenge the children to count how many times they can do it in a row.

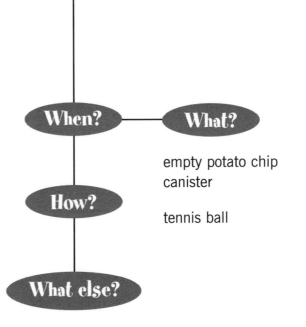

When?

How?

What?

empty potato chip canister

tennis ball

What else?

- Give several children cans. Let them take turns bouncing the ball as their friends try to catch it. The one to catch the ball gets to bounce it the next time.
- Have children paint their cans or cover them with wallpaper scraps.

HINT:

Tennis centers may donate old tennis balls to your classroom.

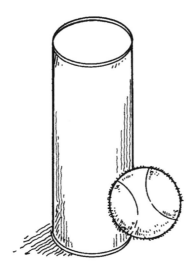

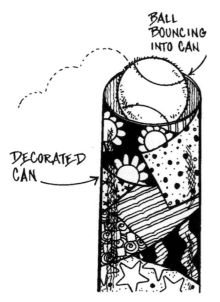

BALL BOUNCING INTO CAN

DECORATED CAN

Windup Key

When?

This prop encourages children to use their imaginations and to move in creative ways.

What? ———— **How?**

heavy cardboard

scissors

aluminum foil

- Trace around the shape of a key on the cardboard.
- Cut it out, then cover with aluminum foil.
- Explain that it is a "magic" key, and when you wind them up they can pretend to be something new.
- Here are some imaginary things they could be:

Hopping bunnies	Chugging trains
Flying eagles	Tiptoeing mice
Dancing snowflakes	Silly clowns
Astronauts on the moon	Marching soldiers
Mad monsters	Twirling leaves

- Slowly walk around the room as you take the key and pretend to wind up children on their backs.

What Else?

- Adapt movement activities to themes, stories, seasons, or holidays.
- Let children take turns winding up their friends with the key.

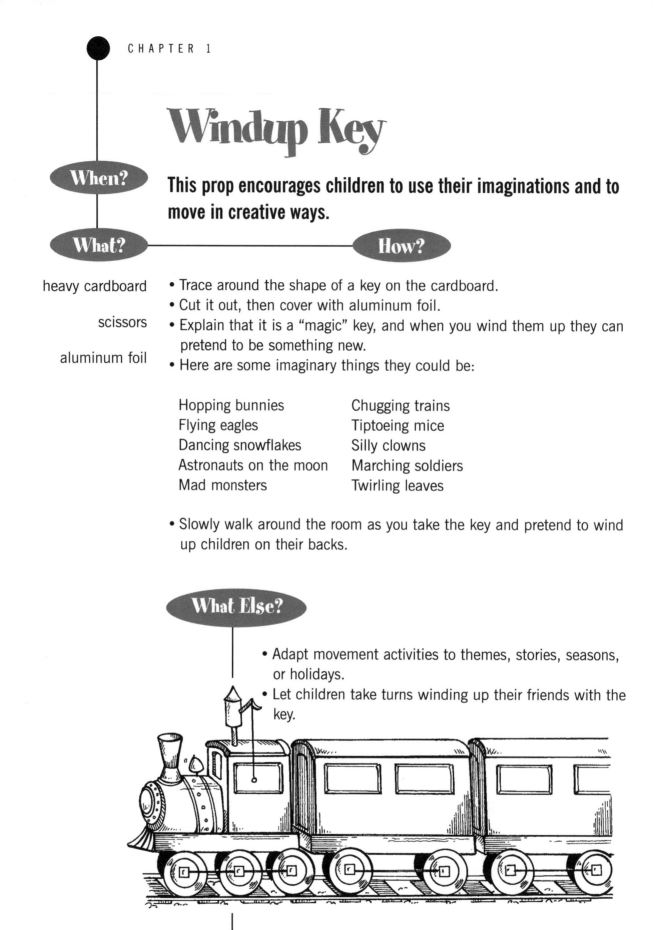

Balance Beam

Develop motor skills and coordination on a rainy day with this imaginary balance beam.

- Place the masking tape on the floor to make a 10' (4 m) line.
- Ask children to line up and tell them to pretend the tape is like a tightrope act in the circus. Have them slowly walk across it one at a time.
- The second time, challenge them to walk backwards across the tape.
- The third time, ask them to try to hop forwards on one foot.
- If appropriate, continue making the task more difficult by having them walk on tip toes, close their eyes, keep their hands by their sides, and so on.

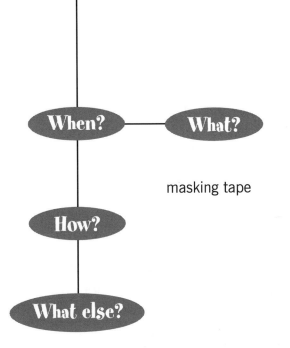

When?   **What?**

masking tape

How?

What else?

- Put the tape on the floor in the shape of an "S," an "8," a triangle, or other letters and geometric shapes.
- Lay a jump rope on the ground out on the playground to make a balance beam game.
- Use a piece of lumber on the floor as a balance beam after the children have mastered the masking tape.

Crossover Movement

When?

There is a line down the middle of the body, and any time we cross over that line, we "unstick" the brain. This activity will not only stimulate the brain, but also provide children with an outlet for wiggles.

What?

How?

roll of toilet paper

variety of music

- Tear off a piece of toilet paper 18"-24" (46 cm-60 cm) long for each child.
- Ask the children to find their own space by extending their arms and turning in a circle.
- Remind children to stay in their space so they don't hit anyone else.
- Put on some music, and ask the children to do what you do.
- Hold the end of your streamer in one hand and begin making circles in front of your body. Make figure eights in front of you. Hold the streamer in your other hand and repeat.
- Make other motions with your streamer as the children follow along.

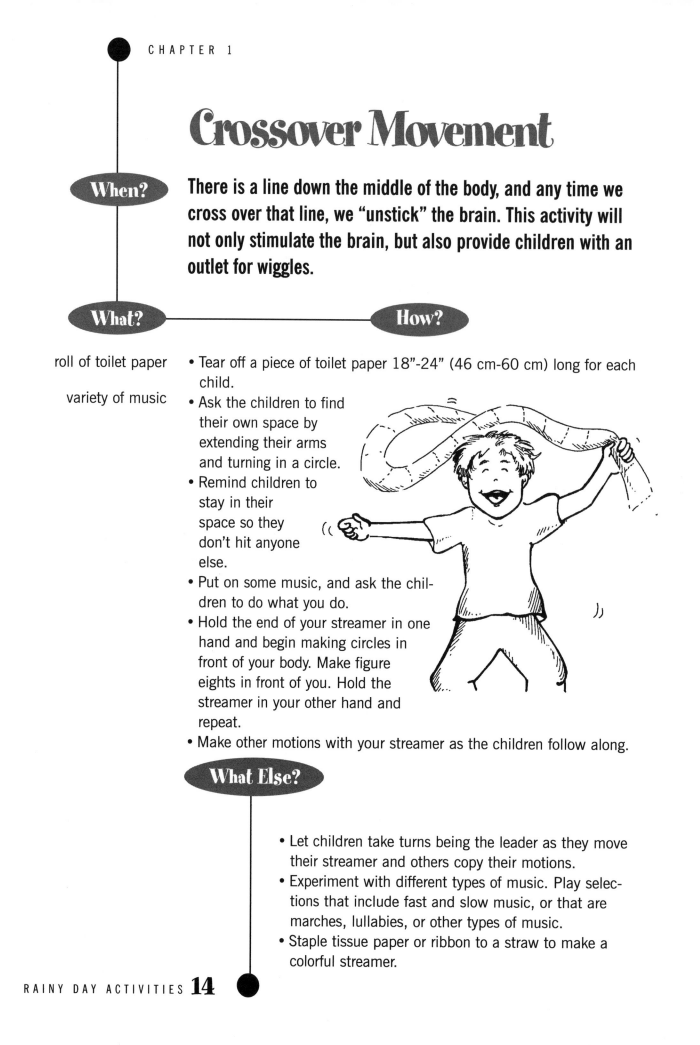

What Else?

- Let children take turns being the leader as they move their streamer and others copy their motions.
- Experiment with different types of music. Play selections that include fast and slow music, or that are marches, lullabies, or other types of music.
- Staple tissue paper or ribbon to a straw to make a colorful streamer.

Jack Be Nimble

Jumping like "Jack" is fun on rainy days or any day!

- Sit in a circle.
- Place the block on the floor in the middle of the circle, and ask the children to pretend it's a candlestick.
- One at a time use children's names in the rhyme below. That child may jump over the block forwards, then backwards, as you say the rhyme.

> (Child's name) be nimble.
> (Child's name) be quick.
> (Child's name) jump over (child jumps forwards)
> The candlestick.
>
> Jump it lively,
> Jump it quick.
> But don't knock over (child jumps backwards)
> The candlestick!

When?

What?

small block

How?

HINT!

Adapt the game to the ability of the children. Young children may only be able to jump forwards. Challenge older children by stacking several blocks.

Sunshine Band

Chase away the clouds and rain with your very own sunshine band. The noise may wake up the whole school, but marching is a good way to stimulate the brain.

What?   **How?**

newspaper or newsprint

markers, crayons, or paper scraps and glue

musical instruments

lively music

• Make a paper hat for each child from newspaper or newsprint, following the directions below.
• To decorate the hats use crayons, markers, or art scraps and glue.
• Next, have each child choose a musical instrument. (If you don't have enough to go around, give them blocks to tap, or two paper plates to use like cymbals.)
• Let the children put on their hats and march around the room as you play some lively music or sing the song below.

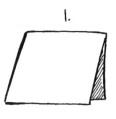

I.

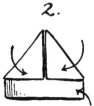

2.

PAPER BOTTOM

3.

FOLD UP
(BOTH SIDES)

4.

DECORATED
HAT

Sunshine Band (Tune: "Old MacDonald")
(Teacher's name) had a band.
E I E I O.
And we are that Sunshine Band.
E I E I O.
So all join in,
Put on a grin.
We're on our way.
It's a happy day.
We are the Sunshine Band.
E I E I O.

What Else?

• March around the halls of your school and add a little novelty and joy to the other classes!

Jukebox

Keep this jukebox handy for when you need a movement song or chant to release energy.

- Cover the box with construction paper.
- Decorate with musical notes and write "Jukebox" on it.
- Cut out words to the titles of movement songs, such as "Hokey Pokey" or "If You're Happy and You Know It" and glue the words in the title of one song to each index card. (Or you can write the title of one song on each index card.)
- Place the cards in the box.
- Whenever you have a few extra minutes, spin a tune on the jukebox.
- Hand a child a pretend quarter. Instruct her to put it in the box and pull out a song.
- The class then sings that song.

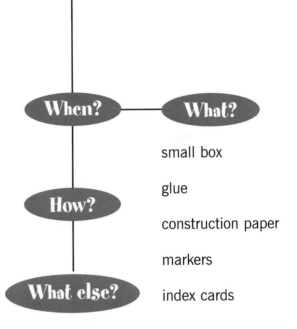

When?

What?

small box

How?

glue

construction paper

markers

What else?

index cards

- You can continue giving children "quarters" and singing the songs they select as long as they are interested.
- Cut paper in the shape of CDs and write the titles of the songs on them.
- Make a similar activity using nursery rhymes.

Hint!

Make copies of the songs in this book and use them in the jukebox.

One-Minute Dramas

When?

Enhance children's imaginations and creativity with these one-minute dramas.

What?   **How?**

wooden chopsticks, cardboard roller from a pants hanger, or wooden dowel

glue

glitter

• Dip the end of the stick or cardboard roller in glue, then roll it in glitter to make a magic wand.
• Explain to the children that you will describe a scene. When you wave your magic wand over them, they will become part of the scene.
• Make up short scenarios similar to the following.

Going on a picnic
Caterpillars turning into butterflies
Autumn leaves falling down
Ducklings hatching from eggs
Merry-go-round horses moving up and down
Going to a birthday party
Popcorn popping
Ice-skaters skating
Riding a bicycle
Being a clown in the circus
Dogs fetching a bone
Flowers growing
Astronauts floating in space
Pancakes cooking
Robots moving
Taking a bath
Eating juicy watermelon
Making a snowman
Getting lost in a store
Riding a magic carpet

Firecracker Boom!

Play this game when it's raining or any time to develop skills and concepts.

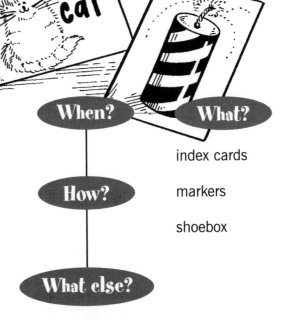

When?

What?

How?

index cards

markers

shoebox

- Choose a concept or theme that you are working on, such as letters, numerals, shapes, or sight words.
- Write the information on the index cards and place the cards face down in the shoebox. (Make sure to make as many cards as there are children in your class.)
- Draw firecrackers similar to the one on this page on three additional cards and put them in the box. Shake up the box.
- Sit in a circle and begin passing around the box.
- Each child will draw a card and identify the information on it. (If they don't know what it is, have the group help them.)
- When a child draws a card with the fire cracker, they say, "Blast off!" and everyone jumps up and claps their hands over their heads as they say, "Boom!"
- The game continues until everyone has had a turn. Collect the cards, shuffle them, and play again!

What else?

- Make new versions of this game to reflect different skills that need to be reinforced.

Juggling

When?

Juggling is a great way to exercise the mind and the body. It's also extra fun on a rainy day to release energy.

What?

How?

several yards of netting (sold at fabric stores) in different colors

scissors

basket

music

- To make juggling scarves, cut the netting into 12" (30 cm) squares. (You will need two for each child.)
- Place the squares in the basket.
- To begin juggling, pass out one scarf to each child. Challenge them to throw their scarves up in the air and catch them. Let the children practice.
- Put on slow, classical music for them to juggle with.
- When children are able to juggle with one scarf let them try it with two. Demonstrate how to "Throw, throw, catch, catch," in a figure eight.

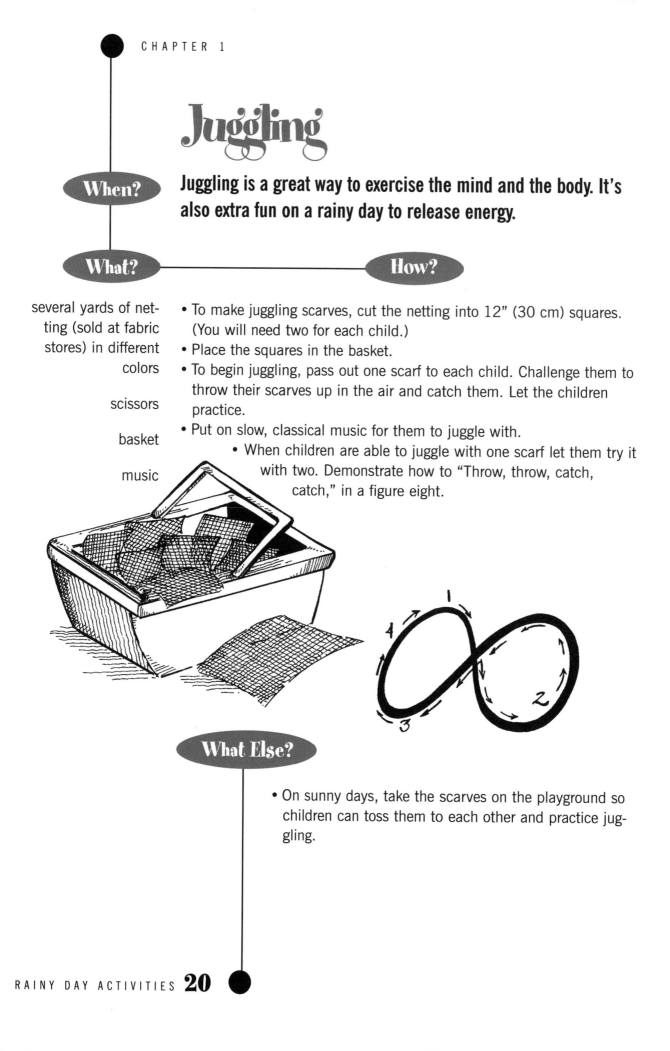

What Else?

- On sunny days, take the scarves on the playground so children can toss them to each other and practice juggling.

Blue Bird

This wonderful old song and game is great for a rainy day and even more fun with this little puppet.

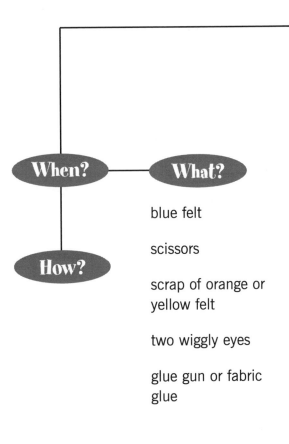

When?

What?

How?

blue felt

scissors

scrap of orange or yellow felt

two wiggly eyes

glue gun or fabric glue

- Use the pattern to make a bird puppet. Cut two bodies and one pair of wings from the felt. Cut a beak out of orange or yellow felt.
- Glue the beak on one section of the body as indicated.
- Spread glue around the outside edge of this piece, leaving an opening of about 1½" (3.5 cm) on the bottom to insert your finger. Place the other section of the body on top.
- Cut a slit through the top of both pieces of the body, as shown. Gather wings, slip them through the slit, then open them up.
- Glue on eyes.
- Have the children stand in a circle holding hands.
- Begin the song by putting the blue bird on your finger. Weave it in and out of the children's arms, or flap your arms like a bird if you do not have a bird puppet.

Blue Bird Through My Window (Traditional Tune)
　　Blue bird, blue bird,
　　Through my window.
　　Blue bird, blue bird,
　　Through my window.
　　Blue bird, blue bird,
　　Through my window,
　　Oh, (child's name), (say child's name you are near)
　　I'm so tired.

　　Find a little friend (tap the puppet on that child's shoulder)
　　And tap them on the shoulder.
　　Find a little friend
　　And tap them on the shoulder.

Find a little friend (pass puppet to that child who exchanges places with you)
And tap them on the shoulder.
Oh, (child's name),
I'm so tired.

- Continue the song with the child using the bird puppet.

What Else?

• This puppet can also be used to "peck" children to dismiss them to a new activity.
• Use the blue bird to help children track a line of print.

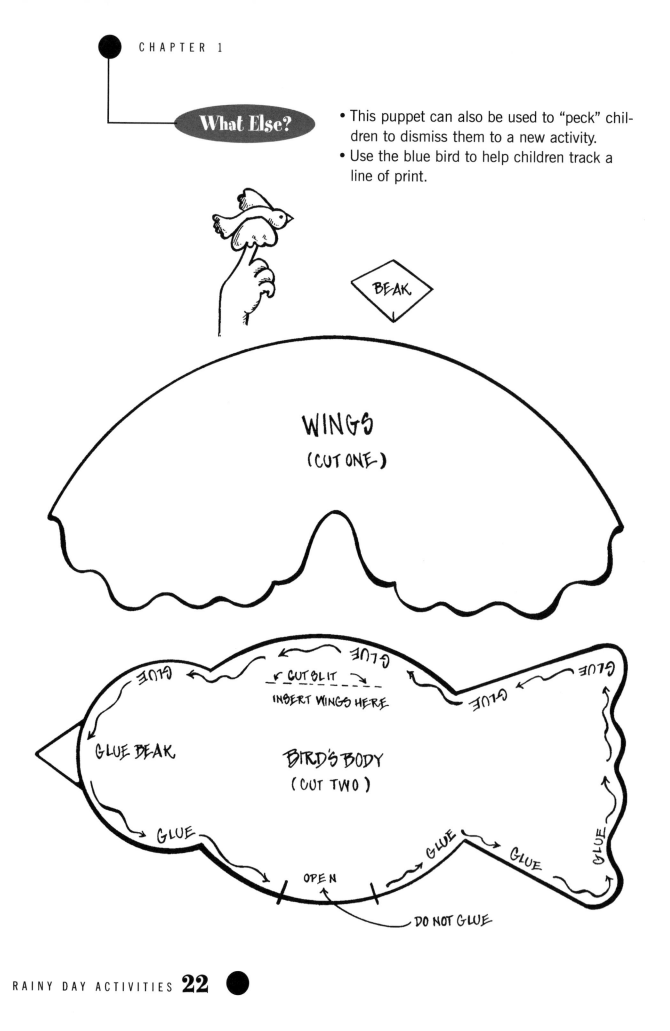

BEAK

WINGS
(CUT ONE)

GLUE
CUT SLIT
INSERT WINGS HERE
GLUE
GLUE
GLUE
GLUE BEAK
BIRD'S BODY
(CUT TWO)
GLUE
GLUE
GLUE
OPEN
GLUE
DO NOT GLUE

Four Corners

Get children up and moving with this game.

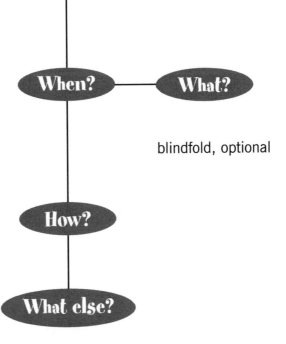

When?

What?

blindfold, optional

How?

What else?

- Number each of the corners in the room—1, 2, 3, and 4.
- Choose one person to be "it."
- She hides her eyes or wears a blindfold for the whole game.
- As "it" slowly counts from one to ten, everyone else tiptoes to a corner in the room.
- When "it" says, "freeze" after counting to ten, everyone must be in a corner.
- "It" then calls out a number (1, 2, 3, or 4) and the children in that corner are out of the game. They sit down in the "stew pot" in the middle of the room.
- "It" counts to ten again as everyone moves to a new corner.
- The game continues until there is one person left. That person becomes the new "it."

- Shorten the games by having "it" call out two corners at a time.

Jumping Beans

Children get to jump and jiggle as they learn.

When?

What? ————————— **How?**

large, empty bean can with label on (Be sure top edge is smooth. Cover with cloth tape if necessary.)

poster board or heavy paper

scissors

markers

- Cut poster board into 6" x 1½" (15 cm x 3.5 cm) strips. Make at least one for each child in the class.
- On the bottom of five strips draw a little bean.
- On the bottom of the other strips draw letters, numerals, shapes, and so on.
- Put all the strips in the bean can, drawing side down.
- Ask the children to sit in a circle.
- One at a time, the children take a strip out of the can and identify the information at the bottom.
- If a child draws a bean, he calls out "Jumping Beans!"
- Everyone stands up and jumps up and down.
- Continue with the next child's turn.

What Else?

- Vary the information on the strips to reinforce a concept or a theme that the children are learning.

No Materials Needed

Row Your Boat

When?

Children will release energy as they develop motor skills and coordination with this game.

What?

How?

no materials needed

- Ask the children to choose a partner and sit on the floor facing their partner with their legs extended.
- The partners touch the bottoms of their feet and hold hands.
- Show them how to slowly move back and forth with their partner as they sing the song below:

  Row, Row, Row Your Boat (Traditional Tune)
  Row, row, row your boat,
  Gently down the stream.
  Merrily, merrily, merrily, merrily,
  Life is but a dream.

- Continue singing the song slowly until children catch on to the rhythm and are moving in unison.

What Else?

- Tell them to turn up their engines and be motorboats as you sing the song a little faster.
- Sing the song at different speeds and ask the children to move accordingly.

London Bridge

This game requires no special skills and is a favorite of children of all ages. Although it has been around for years, the game is new, fresh, and exciting for children who have never experienced it.

- Choose two children to be the bridge. They face each other.
- Show them how to hold hands and extend their arms in the air.
- The other children line up and walk in single file under the bridge as you sing:

  London Bridge (Traditional Tune)
  London Bridge is falling down,
  Falling down, falling down.
  London Bridge is falling down,
  My fair lady. (the two bridge children bring their arms down and "capture" another child)

  Take the keys and lock her up, (the bridge children gently swing this third child back and forth)
  Lock her up, lock her up.
  Take the keys and lock her up,
  My fair lady.

- The child who was "caught" takes the place of one child who was part of the bridge and the game continues.

When? **What?**

no materials needed

How?

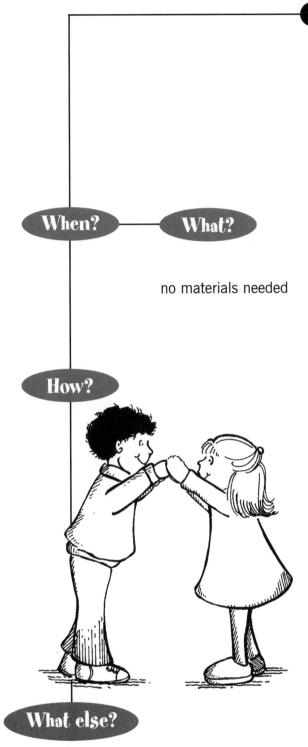

What else?

- Children who are caught stand behind one of the two children who are the bridge until all the children are "caught."

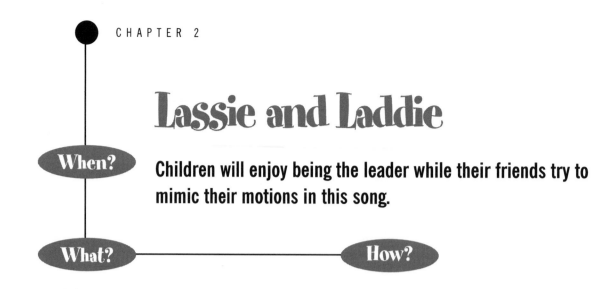

Lassie and Laddie

When?

Children will enjoy being the leader while their friends try to mimic their motions in this song.

What?

How?

no materials needed

Explain to the children that in Scotland boys are called laddies and girls are called lassies.

• Ask the children to stand in a circle, then choose a girl to get in the middle.

• Ask everyone if the child in the middle is a lassie or laddie, then sing the song below as the child in the middle jumps, hops, dances, or another motion of her choice. The other children mimic the motions of the child in the middle.

Did You Ever See a Lassie? (Traditional Tune)
Did you ever see a lassie,
A lassie, a lassie?
Did you ever see a lassie
Go this way and that?
Go this way, and that way,
And this way, and that way.
Did you ever see a lassie
Go this way and that?

The lassie (girl) in the middle then chooses a laddie (boy) to take her place, as you sing:

Did you ever see a laddie,
A laddie, a laddie...

• The game continues until all children have had a turn being lassie or laddie.

Singing the ABCs

Try these creative, new versions of the traditional alphabet song to sing on rainy days or any day!

When?

What?

no materials needed

How?

• Slowly sing the "Alphabet Song" using one of these ideas:

The Alphabet Song (Traditional Tune)
A B C D E F G H I J K L M N O P
Q R S T U V W X Y Z
Now I've said my ABC's,
Next time won't you sing with me?

Monster version—Sing with a loud voice.
Mouse version—Sing with a high, squeaky voice.
Opera version—Sing dramatically with out-stretched arms.
Backwards version—Turn around and sing.
Upside down version—Put head on the floor and sing.
With a cold version—Hold nose and sing.
Underwater version—Put finger between lips and wiggle.
Z Y X version—Sing backwards from Z to A— very hard!).
Silent version—Mouth the words with no sound.

Hint!

Be sure to enunciate each letter distinctly so they don't blend together.

Alphabet Chant

When?

Try this chant to get children up and moving.

What?

How?

no materials needed

- Begin marching and slapping your arms on your sides as you say the chant below.

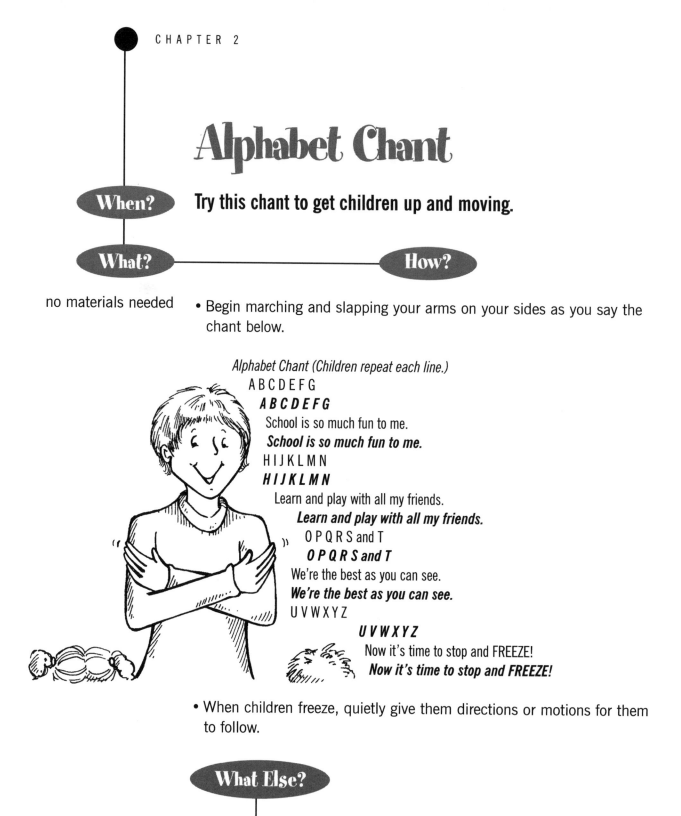

Alphabet Chant (Children repeat each line.)
A B C D E F G
A B C D E F G
School is so much fun to me.
School is so much fun to me.
H I J K L M N
H I J K L M N
Learn and play with all my friends.
Learn and play with all my friends.
O P Q R S and T
O P Q R S and T
We're the best as you can see.
We're the best as you can see.
U V W X Y Z
U V W X Y Z
Now it's time to stop and FREEZE!
Now it's time to stop and FREEZE!

- When children freeze, quietly give them directions or motions for them to follow.

What Else?

- Change the last words of the chant to say, "Now, look at your teacher, please;" "Now walk quietly, please;" "Now get on your coats, please;" or whatever else you want them to do.

Nursery Rhyme Time

Early literacy research suggests a positive correlation between children's ability to rhyme and their ability to read.

• Act out the nursery rhymes below to fill bits and pieces of time during the day.

> Humpty Dumpty sat on a wall,
> Humpty Dumpty had a great fall.
> All the king's horses,
> And all the king's men,
> Couldn't put Humpty together again.

> Little Miss Muffet sat on a tuffet,
> Eating her curds and whey.
> Along came a spider and sat down beside her,
> And frightened Miss Muffet away.

> Jack and Jill went up the hill
> To fetch a pail of water.
> Jack fell down,
> And broke his crown,
> And Jill came tumbling after.

> Hey, Diddle, Diddle, the cat and the fiddle
> The cow jumped over the moon.
> The little dog laughed to see such a sport.
> And the dish ran away with the spoon.

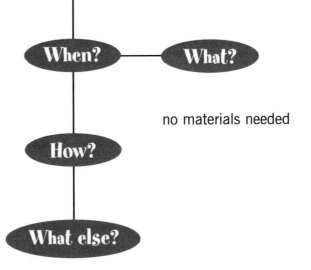

When? — **What?**

no materials needed

How?

What else?

• Try singing the rhymes to the tune of "100 Bottles of Beer on the Wall." Give it a try! You'll be surprised!

Bubble Gum

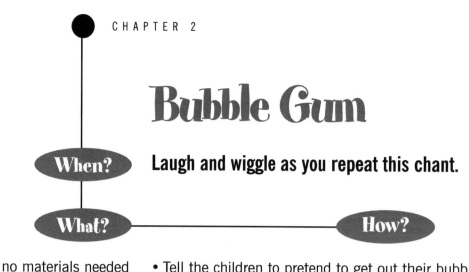

Laugh and wiggle as you repeat this chant.

no materials needed

- Tell the children to pretend to get out their bubble gum, unwrap it, put it in their mouths and begin to chew.

Bubble Gum

> Bubble gum, bubble gum, (roll hands around)
> Sticky, sticky, sticky, bubble gum,
> And it sticks right to my head. (put hands on head and pretend to pull away)
> So I pull,
> And I pull,
> And I PULL! (pull free of head)

- Pretend to stick bubble gum to other body parts, such as your stomach, feet, face, etc.
- End by having the children pretend to put their bubble gum back in the wrapper and throw it away in the trash can.

Let's Make Music!

Make music throughout the day with this movement chant.

- Sit on the floor and model what you want the children to do as you chant:

Let's Make Music
> Let's make music with our hands,
> Clap, clap, clap. (clap 3 times)
> Let's make music with our hands,
> Clap, clap, clap. (clap 3 times)
> Let's make music with our hands,
> Let's make music with our hands,
> Let's make music with our hands,
> Clap, clap, clap. (clap 3 times)
>
> Let's make music with our fingers,
> Snap, snap, snap… (snap 3 times)
>
> Let's make music with our feet,
> Tap, tap, tap… (tap feet 3 times)
>
> We can put them all together
> Clap, snap, tap… (clap, snap, and tap)

- Sing the chant to "She'll Be Comin' Around the Mountain."

When? — **What?**

no materials needed

How?

What else?

- Ask children to suggest other ways they can make sounds with their bodies. For example, lips could smack, tongues could click, feet could stomp, and so on.
- Pass out musical instruments and ask children to play them as you chant about the different instruments. For example, "Let's make music with the sticks…"

Popcorn

When?

Children will have to listen and respond to this poem.

What?

no materials needed

How?

- Ask the children if they've ever seen popcorn popping in a pan. What happens? Explain that they get to be like little popcorn kernels.
- Every time they hear the word "Pop!" they get to jump up and clap their hands over their heads.
- Begin by asking the children to squat down on the floor and repeat this rhyme with you.

Popcorn
Five little kernels sizzling in the pot.
The grease got hot and one went "Pop!" (children jump up)

Four little kernels sizzling in the pot.
The grease got hot and one went "Pop!" (children jump up)

Three...
Two...
One...

No little kernels sizzling in the pot.
The pot got hot and it went "Pop!" (children jump up)

What Else?

- Have the children hold their hands and say this rhyme with you. They can clap their hands on the word "Pop!"

Let's Do a Little Twirling

Children naturally stimulate their brains as they wiggle and play. Twirling, jumping, rocking, marching, and other gross motor movements are other enjoyable ways to exercise the brain (and the body).

- Remind the children how important it is to exercise and how much their brains love to move. Demonstrate each of the verses, with the children following along.

  Let's Do a Little Twirling (Tune: "We Wish You a Merry Christmas")
      Let's all do a little twirling, (children stand and slowly spin around)
      Let's all do a little twirling,
      Let's all do a little twirling,
      To exercise our brains.

- Insert the following words in the song. Do the motions as you sing the song.

      Hopping
      Jumping
      Marching
      Rocking
      Running
      Swimming

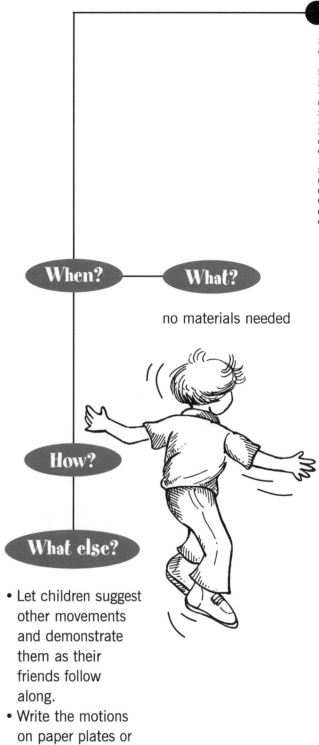

When? **What?**

no materials needed

How?

What else?

- Let children suggest other movements and demonstrate them as their friends follow along.
- Write the motions on paper plates or strips of poster board. Hold them up as you sing them.

There Was a Wise Teacher

When?

Use this version of an old song to exercise children on a rainy day (or any day!).

What? ──────────── **How?**

no materials needed

• Have the children stand up and do what you do:

There Was a Wise Teacher (Tune: "The Noble Duke of York")
   There was a wise teacher. (begin marching in place and swinging your arms)
   She had so many children.
   She marched them up the hall,
   And she marched them down again. (stoop down)
   And when you're up, you're up. (stand up tall)
   And when you're down, you're down. (stoop down)
   And when you're only halfway up, (bend knees slightly)
   You're neither up, nor down. (stand up, then down)

• Sing the song slowly and move accordingly.
• Sing fast and move quickly.
• Mouth the words as you do the motions.

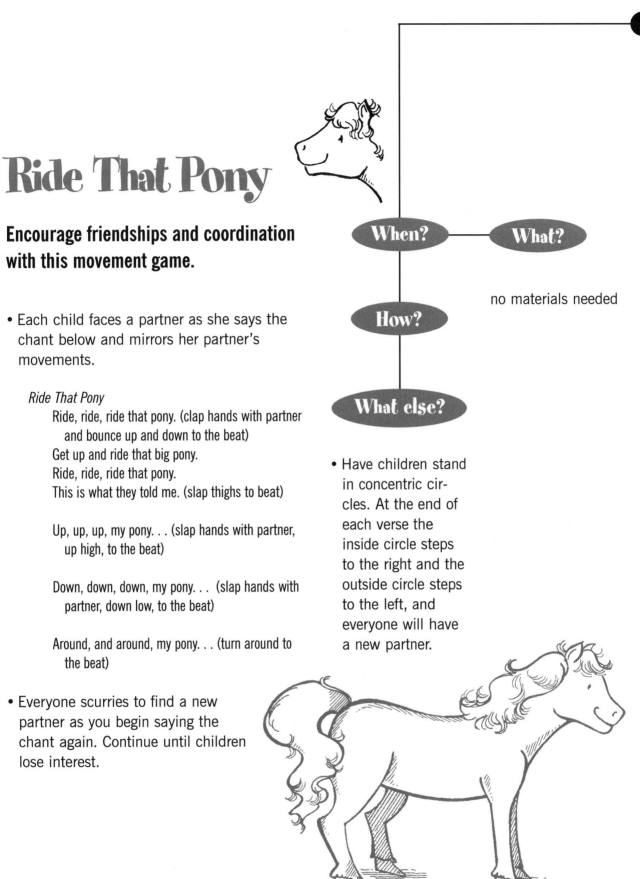

Ride That Pony

Encourage friendships and coordination with this movement game.

When?   **What?**

How?

no materials needed

What else?

• Each child faces a partner as she says the chant below and mirrors her partner's movements.

Ride That Pony
    Ride, ride, ride that pony. (clap hands with partner and bounce up and down to the beat)
    Get up and ride that big pony.
    Ride, ride, ride that pony.
    This is what they told me. (slap thighs to beat)

    Up, up, up, my pony. . . (slap hands with partner, up high, to the beat)

    Down, down, down, my pony. . . (slap hands with partner, down low, to the beat)

    Around, and around, my pony. . . (turn around to the beat)

• Everyone scurries to find a new partner as you begin saying the chant again. Continue until children lose interest.

• Have children stand in concentric circles. At the end of each verse the inside circle steps to the right and the outside circle steps to the left, and everyone will have a new partner.

Chugga Chugga

When?

Here's another movement chant children will beg to do over and over.

What?

How?

no materials needed

• Have children stand in a line behind you as you begin saying the chant and modeling the movements.

Chugga Chugga Chant
Ms. (Teacher's name) (clap hands and move side to side)
Has a real cool class.
They've got a lot of this, (stick out pointer finger on each hand and dance)
And a lot of that.
So come on now and get up, (shake pointer fingers up in the air to the beat)
Chugga-chugga-chugga,
Chugga-chug-chug.
Get down chugga-chugga, (shake pointer fingers down to the floor)
Chugga-chug-chug.
To the left chugga-chugga, (shake fingers as you slide to the left)
Chugga-chug-chug.
To the right chugga-chugga, (shake fingers as you slide to the right)
Chugga-chug-chug.

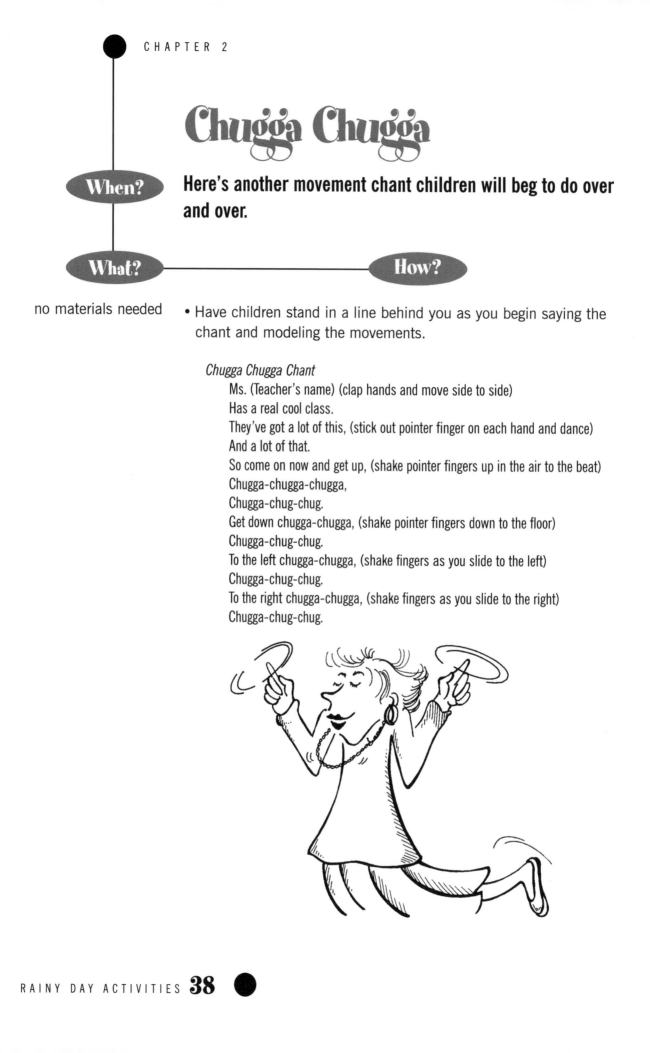

Robots

As children pretend to be robots they develop large motor skills and coordination.

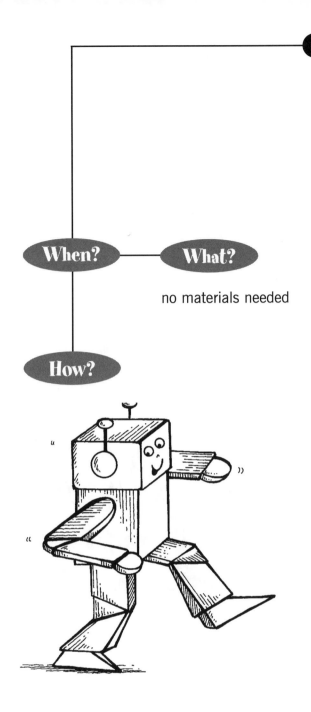

When? — **What?**

no materials needed

How?

- Have children stand and follow along as you say the chant below in a mechanical, staccato voice.

Robots
>What would you do if you went to robot school?
>Just look at me, and a robot you will be.
>Robots at attention. (stand at attention)
>Robots, let's begin.
>Right arm. (start moving right arm up and down)
>
>What would you do if you went to robot school?
>Just look at me, and a robot you will be.
>Robots at attention. (stand at attention)
>Robots, let's begin.
>Right arm. (start moving right arm up and down)
>Left arm. (move left arm up and down, too)

- Continue, adding the following motions:

>Right foot. (move right foot up and down)
>Left foot. (move left foot up and down)
>Head up. Head down. (move head up and down)
>Tongue in. Tongue out. (stick tongue in and out)
>Turn around. (turn around as you do the other motions)
>Robots sit down. (end chant by having children sit down)

Mother Goony Bird

When?

Wiggle and chant any time during the day with Mother Goony Bird.

What?   **How?**

no materials needed

• Have children stand and follow along as you chant and make the motions below:

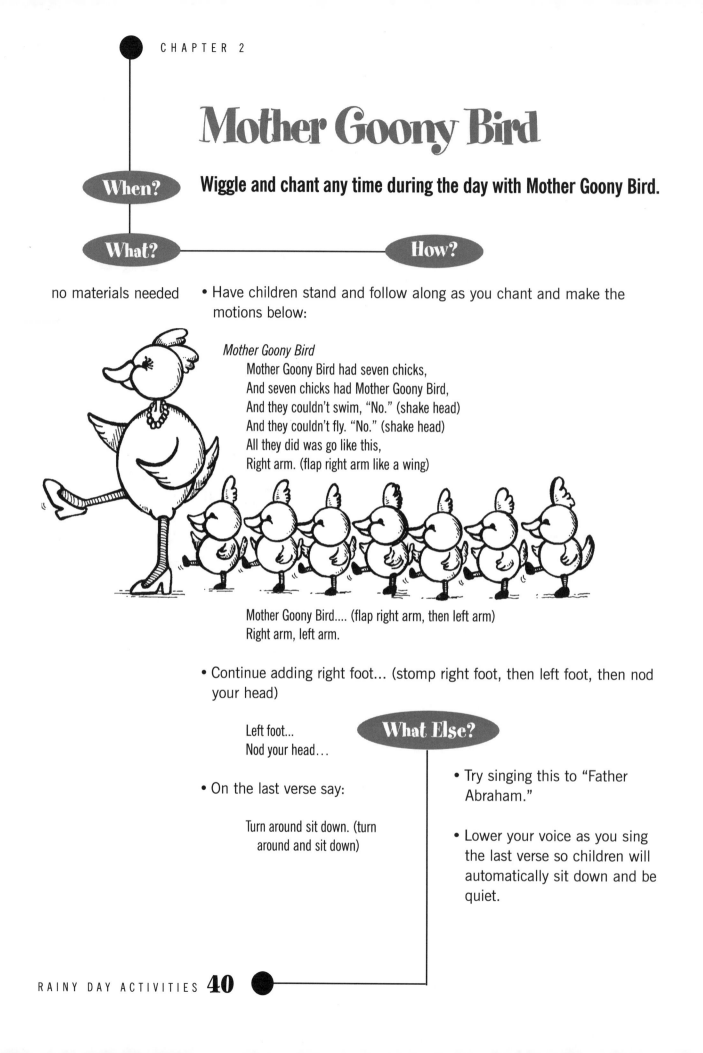

Mother Goony Bird
Mother Goony Bird had seven chicks,
And seven chicks had Mother Goony Bird,
And they couldn't swim, "No." (shake head)
And they couldn't fly. "No." (shake head)
All they did was go like this,
Right arm. (flap right arm like a wing)

Mother Goony Bird.... (flap right arm, then left arm)
Right arm, left arm.

• Continue adding right foot... (stomp right foot, then left foot, then nod your head)

Left foot...
Nod your head…

What Else?

• On the last verse say:

Turn around sit down. (turn around and sit down)

• Try singing this to "Father Abraham."

• Lower your voice as you sing the last verse so children will automatically sit down and be quiet.

Hello, Neighbor!

Brain research emphasizes the importance of using rituals and songs. This partner game will also create positive feelings.

When?

What?

no materials needed

How?

What else?

- Demonstrate the chant and movements with a partner.
- Each child gets a partner and slowly repeats the chant and actions.
- Continue chanting the poem, changing partners each time after you turn around.

    Hello, Neighbor!
    Hello, neighbor. (wave to partner)
    What do you say? (give high five)
    It's going to be a happy day. (clap hands)
    Greet your neighbor. (shake hands)
    Boogie on down. (wiggle hips)
    Give a bump, (gently bump hips)
    And turn around. (turn around, then move to a new partner)

- Try singing the poem to the tune of "Good Night, Ladies."

- Begin the song with two children doing the dance while the other children sit on the floor. After chanting one verse, they each select a new partner. After the second round, the four children standing each select a new partner. The chant continues until every child is standing and participating.

Everybody Shake a Hand

When?

Here's a happy tune to create group cohesiveness.

What? How?

no materials needed

• Begin singing the song and modeling what the children are to do:

Everybody Shake a Hand (Tune: "Buffalo Gal")
Everybody shake a hand, (shake children's hands as you walk around the room)
Shake a hand,
Shake a hand.
Everybody shake a hand,
And walk around the room.

Everybody give high five... (slap right hands together in the air)

Everybody scratch a back... (scratch each other's backs)

Everybody give a hug, (end by giving hugs, then sitting down)
Give a hug,
Give a hug.
Everybody give a hug,
And then you take a seat.

What Else?

• Ask the children to suggest verses for different things they could do, such as "bow to a friend," "give a smile," "say hello," "give a bump," etc.

Baby Birds

Lower the noise level with this game that challenges children to listen carefully.

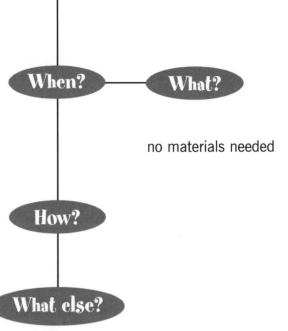

When?

What?

no materials needed

How?

What else?

- Children sit on the floor or in chairs.
- One child is selected to be Mama Bird or Papa Bird. This child leaves the room.
- While this child is out of the room, five other children are chosen to be Baby Birds.
- All the children put their heads down, and the Mama Bird or Papa Bird is called back in the room.
- The Baby Birds then begin "chirping" as Mama or Papa goes around and tries to identify who the baby birds are.
- When all the baby birds have been found, begin another round of the game.

- Use different animals to play this game. Pretend to be puppies, kittens, cubs, and so on.

The Quiet Touch

Enjoy this active game any time of the day.

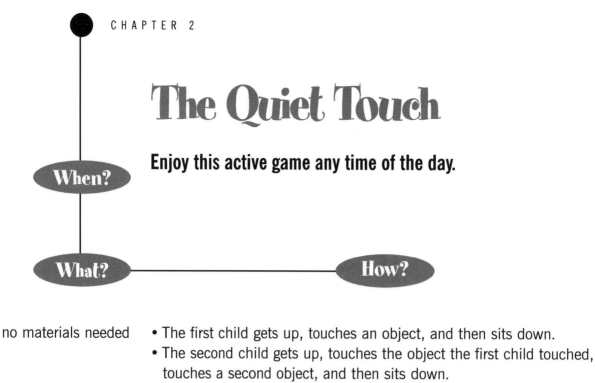

When?

What?

How?

no materials needed

- The first child gets up, touches an object, and then sits down.
- The second child gets up, touches the object the first child touched, touches a second object, and then sits down.
- The game continues with each child touching the objects the previous children touched in sequential order, plus a new object.
- When a child misses an object, just begin a new game.

What Else?

- Play a similar game with noises. When playing Noisy Touch, children might turn on the water, shut the door, write on the board, move a chair, and so on. Each child adds a new sound until the sequence is missed or all the children have had a turn. Then begin again.

Relaxing and Calming Activities

Chapter 3

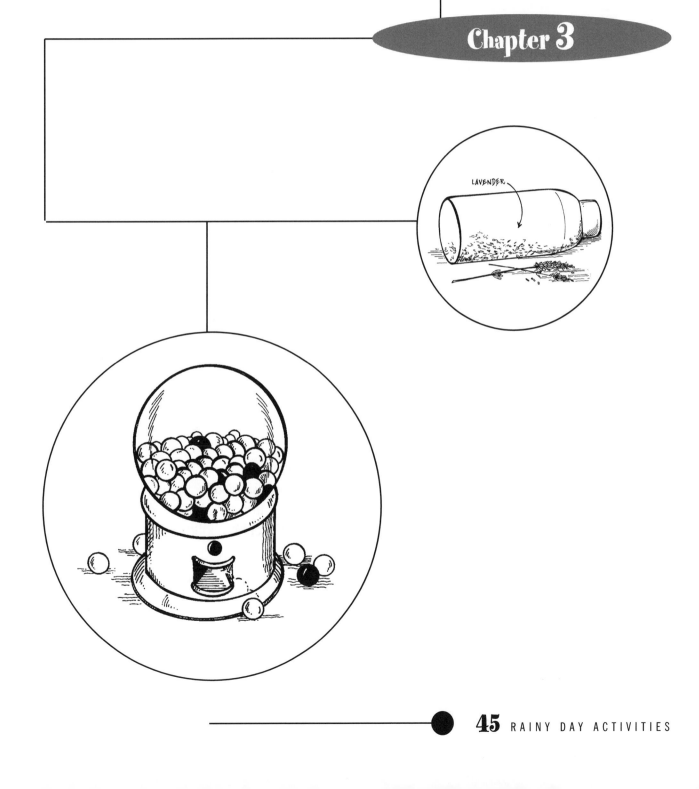

LAVENDER

Mozart-Food for the Brain!

When?

Play Mozart for the children to create a relaxing and positive learning environment.

What?

How?

Mozart recording

tape or CD player

• Play the music softly in the background.
• Ask the children if they notice anything different. Have they ever heard music like that before?

• Tell them that the music was written by Mozart and that you've read that classical music by Mozart and others can help their brains work better.

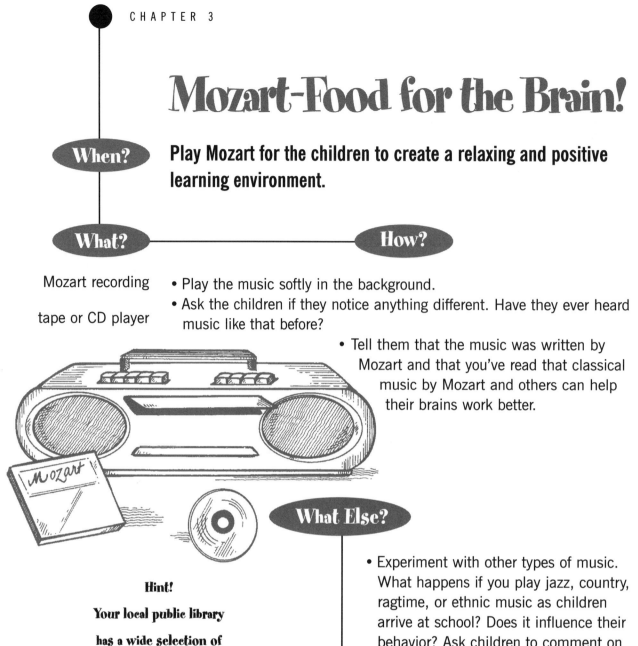

What Else?

Hint!
Your local public library has a wide selection of classical music and many other types of recordings.

• Experiment with other types of music. What happens if you play jazz, country, ragtime, or ethnic music as children arrive at school? Does it influence their behavior? Ask children to comment on how various types of music make them feel.
• Use background music during rest time, independent reading time, or other times during the day and notice the effect on children.

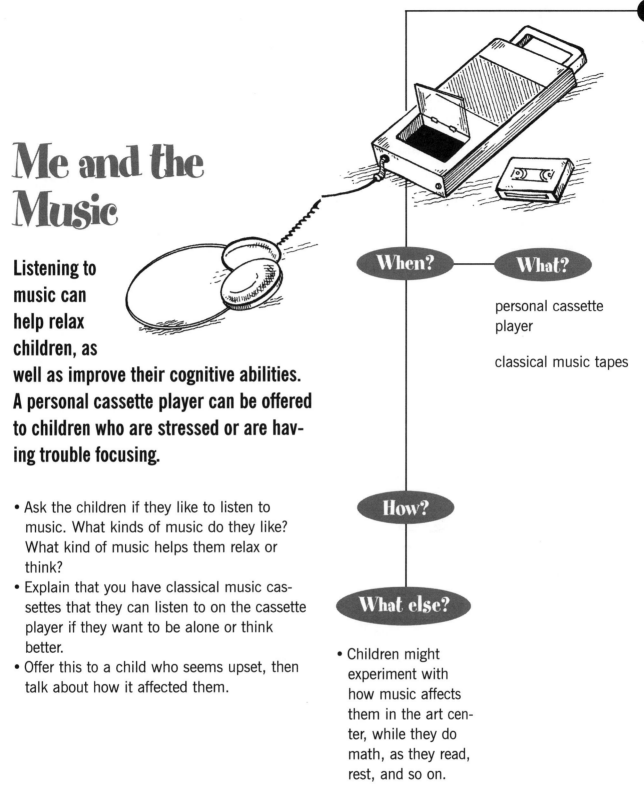

Me and the Music

Listening to music can help relax children, as well as improve their cognitive abilities. A personal cassette player can be offered to children who are stressed or are having trouble focusing.

- Ask the children if they like to listen to music. What kinds of music do they like? What kind of music helps them relax or think?
- Explain that you have classical music cassettes that they can listen to on the cassette player if they want to be alone or think better.
- Offer this to a child who seems upset, then talk about how it affected them.

When?

What?

personal cassette player

classical music tapes

How?

What else?

- Children might experiment with how music affects them in the art center, while they do math, as they read, rest, and so on.

Relax Bottle

When?

This bottle may help children relax, focus, and calm down. (This is a more positive alternative to time out and is often more effective.)

What?

How?

plastic bottle

crayon shavings

water

glue gun or super glue

- Remove the label from the bottle.
- Put several spoonfuls of crayon shavings in the bottle, then fill with water.
- Glue on the lid with a glue gun or super glue.
- If a child is out of control, shake up the bottle and then hand it to the child. Ask him to hold the bottle until all the crayons have stopped moving around.

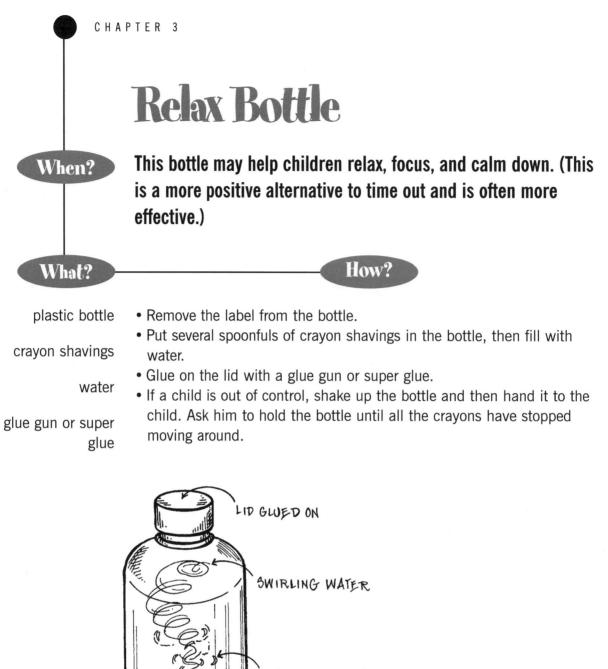

LID GLUED ON

SWIRLING WATER

CRAYON SHAVINGS

Twinkling Stars

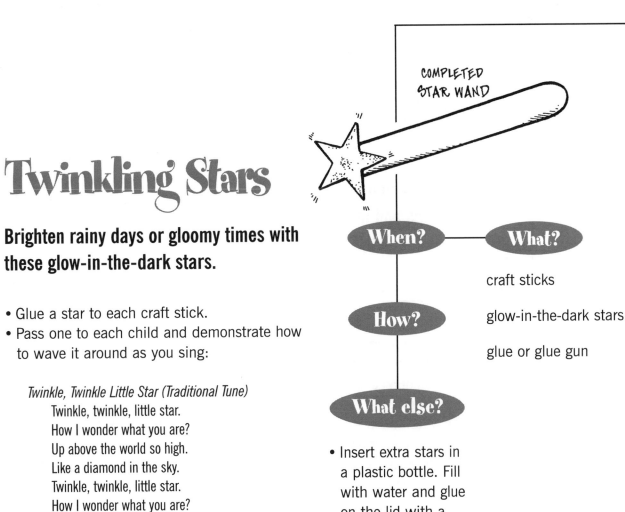

COMPLETED
STAR WAND

Brighten rainy days or gloomy times with these glow-in-the-dark stars.

• Glue a star to each craft stick.
• Pass one to each child and demonstrate how to wave it around as you sing:

> *Twinkle, Twinkle Little Star (Traditional Tune)*
> Twinkle, twinkle, little star.
> How I wonder what you are?
> Up above the world so high.
> Like a diamond in the sky.
> Twinkle, twinkle, little star.
> How I wonder what you are?

• Tell the children that you are going to turn off the lights and close the blinds to darken the room. Explain that something magic will happen to their stars.
• Sing the song again in the dark as the children wave and "twinkle" their stars.

When?

How?

What else?

What?

craft sticks

glow-in-the-dark stars

glue or glue gun

• Insert extra stars in a plastic bottle. Fill with water and glue on the lid with a glue gun. Let a child who is having trouble relaxing play with the bottle.

Hint!
This is a good opportunity to help children who are fearful of the dark by talking about all the fun things you can do when it's dark.

STARS

GLUE

GLUE

CRAFT STICKS

Marshmallow Feet

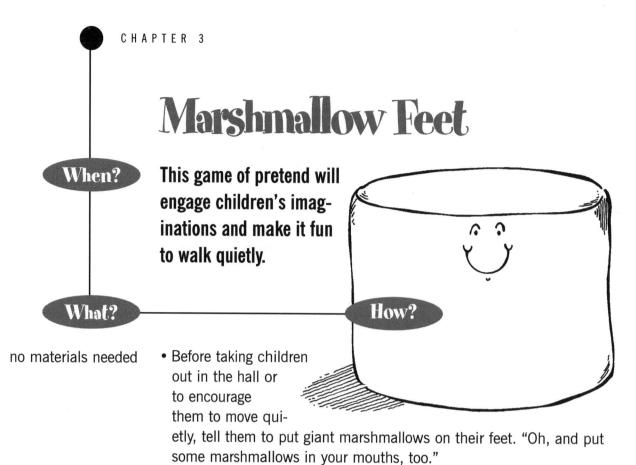

When?

This game of pretend will engage children's imaginations and make it fun to walk quietly.

What?

no materials needed

How?

- Before taking children out in the hall or to encourage them to move quietly, tell them to put giant marshmallows on their feet. "Oh, and put some marshmallows in your mouths, too."
- Model this by puffing up your cheeks and walking dramatically like you have big, fluffy feet.

What Else?

- Make up other imagination games to help children move quietly. For example, you could be like "Stealth jets" and walk so quietly no one else can detect you. Have children suggest other quiet motions.
- When coming in from the playground with dirty shoes, show the children how to go, "One, two, three, cha-cha-cha." As they "cha-cha-cha," they'll be cleaning their shoes!

Listen Please!

Try one of the poems below to calm children.

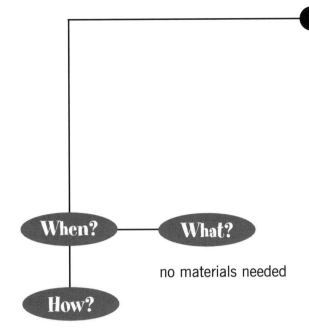

When? **What?**

no materials needed

How?

• Quietly repeat one of these rhymes, lowering your voice as you do so.

We Listen
> We listen with our ears, of course, (point to ears)
> But surely it is true,
> That eyes and lips and hands and feet (point to other parts of the body)
> Can surely listen, too.

Give Yourself a Hug
> Give yourself a great big hug. (hug self)
> Give it all you've got.
> Pat yourself upon the back. (pat back)
> Smile and smile a lot! (smile)

Q-U-I-E-T
> Q (hold up thumb)
> U (hold up index finger)
> I (hold up middle finger)
> E (hold up ring finger)
> T (hold up little finger)
> Quiet, quiet. (wave hand and whisper the last two lines)
> That's what I'll be.

Positive Feedback

When?

Use this "trick" as a positive behavior cue.

What?   **How?**

plastic bottle

clear corn syrup

measuring cup

teaspoon

glitter or seasonal
confetti

food coloring

glue gun

- Pour ½ cup (125 ml) of corn syrup in the bottle.
- Add 1 teaspoon of glitter or seasonal confetti to the bottle, a drop of food coloring, and glue on the lid.
- Hand the bottle to the child who is modeling appropriate behavior and say, "You are doing the right thing."
- Continue doing this throughout the day to reinforce positive behavior.

What Else?

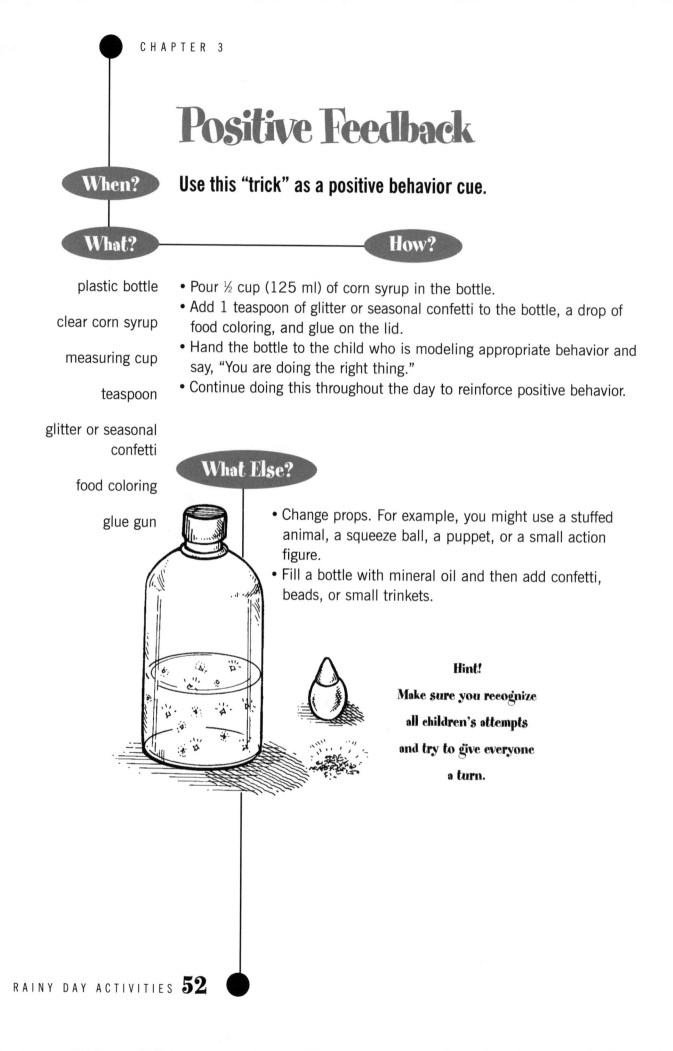

- Change props. For example, you might use a stuffed animal, a squeeze ball, a puppet, or a small action figure.
- Fill a bottle with mineral oil and then add confetti, beads, or small trinkets.

Hint!

Make sure you recognize all children's attempts and try to give everyone a turn.

Wiggle Wobble

Use this chant to release wiggles and focus children's attention.

- Start saying this chant and modeling what you want children to do.

    Wiggle Wobble
    Heads go wiggle, wobble, (wiggle head from side to side)
    Wiggle, wobble,
    Wiggle, wobble.
    Heads go wiggle, wobble,
    Then they STOP! (freeze)

    Fingers go wiggle, wobble, (wiggle fingers)
    Wiggle, wobble,
    Wiggle, wobble.
    Fingers go wiggle, wobble,
    Then they STOP! (freeze with hands in lap)

- Continue using other body parts in the poem as you wiggle them and then "freeze."

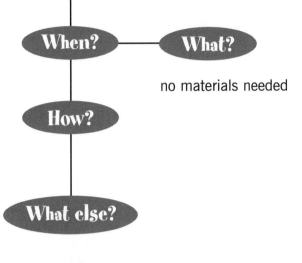

When?

What?

no materials needed

How?

What else?

- Let children suggest other parts of the body they can wiggle.

WIGGLE   STOP   WOBBLE

Stop and Drop

When?

Try this little movement song to focus children's attention.

What?

How?

no materials needed

• Demonstrate the motions as you sing:

Stop and Drop (Tune: "Frere Jacques")
    Running, running, (run in place)
    Running, running,
    Hop, hop, hop, (hop on right foot)
    Hop, hop, hop. (hop on left)
    Tiptoe, tiptoe, (tiptoe)
    Tiptoe, tiptoe.
    Then I stop, (hold up hand)
    And I drop! (sit down on floor)

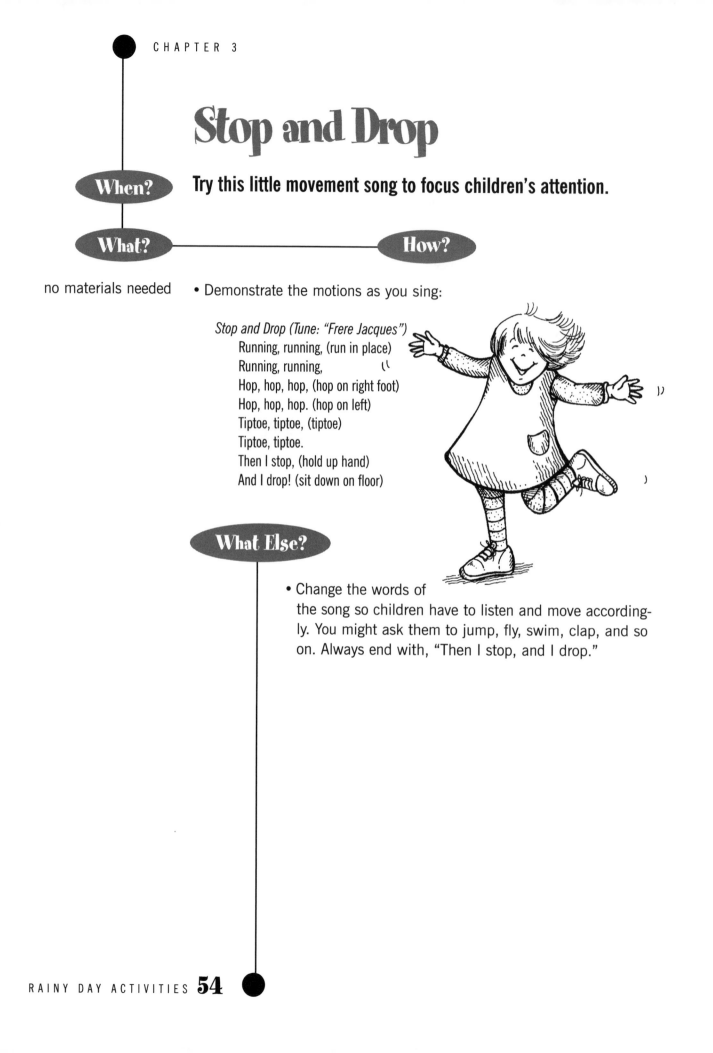

What Else?

• Change the words of
the song so children have to listen and move according-ly. You might ask them to jump, fly, swim, clap, and so on. Always end with, "Then I stop, and I drop."

2-4-6-8-10

Engage all children with this magic clap.

• When helping children relax, say:

Follow me.
   Two (clap two index fingers together)
   Four (clap index and middle fingers together)
   Six (clap index, middle and ring fingers together)
   Eight (clap index, middle, ring, and little fingers together)
   Ten (clap both hands together)

   End by silently putting your hands in your lap.

When? **What?**

How?

no materials needed

What else?

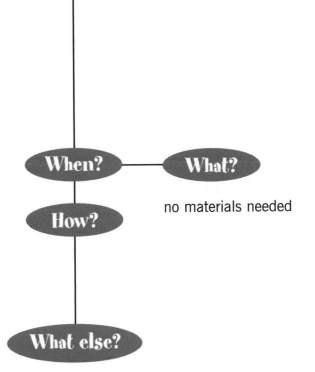

• Do the clap forwards (2-4-6-8-10) and then backwards (10-8-6-4-2-0).
• Use other clapping patterns to focus children. You might say, "Can you do this?" as you begin clapping or snapping a beat.
• Let children think of clapping patterns for their friends to repeat as you wait between activities.

Clocks

When?

Children love the exaggeration of this rhyme, and it's a great way to focus their attention.

What?   **How?**

no materials needed

• Begin this fingerplay by demonstrating how to be a big clock by making a circle above your head with your arms.

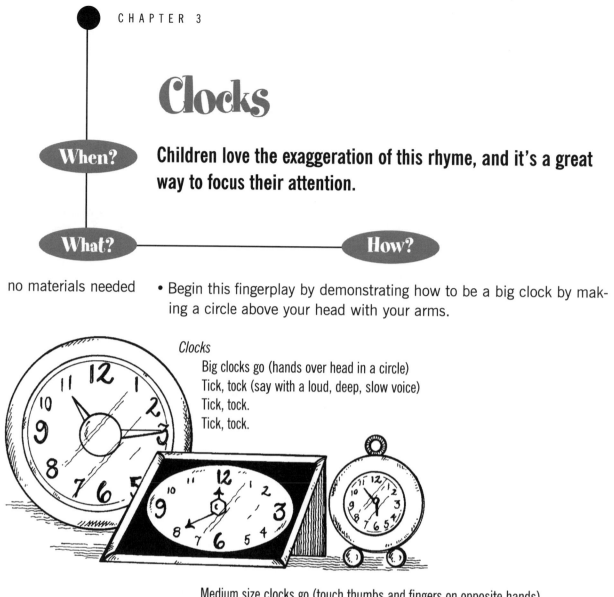

Clocks
Big clocks go (hands over head in a circle)
Tick, tock (say with a loud, deep, slow voice)
Tick, tock.
Tick, tock.

Medium size clocks go (touch thumbs and fingers on opposite hands)
Tick, tock (say in an average voice at a medium speed)
Tick, tock.
Tick, tock.

And little tiny clocks go (make a small circle with index finger and thumb)
Tick, tock (say slowly in a high, squeaky voice)
Tick, tock
Tick, tock

What Else?

• Say other rhymes with a deep voice, high voice, fast, slow, loud, soft, and so on.

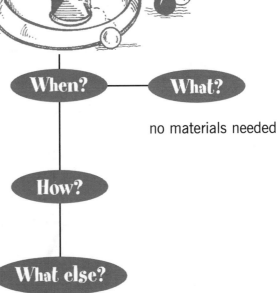

The Gumball

Children will be so engaged with this tongue twister, they won't realize they are developing phonological skills.

When?   **What?**

no materials needed

How?

- Teach the children the chant below:

    The Gumball
    I put the penny in the gum slot.
    I watched the gum roll down.
    I get the gum and you get the wrapper,
    Cause I put the penny in the gum slot.

- Chant it again changing the beginning letter of each word. For example, using "b" the song would go:

    Bi but be benny bin be bum bot.
    Bi batched be bum boll bown.
    Bi bet be bum band bou bet be bapper,
    Bause bi but be benny bin be bum bot.

- Continue inserting different consonants in the tune.

What else?

- Write the song on a language experience chart or overhead projector. Make additional copies of other verses.

Peaceful Spray

When?

Certain aromas have different effects on the brain and body. Lavender or rosemary tends to have a calming affect on behavior, so try this technique on rainy days or when tempers start to flare.

What?

How?

lavender air spray

• When children are acting stressful or aggressive, tell the children that you have some Peaceful Spray to make them feel better.
• Spray the lavender around the room.
• Ask children how it makes them feel.

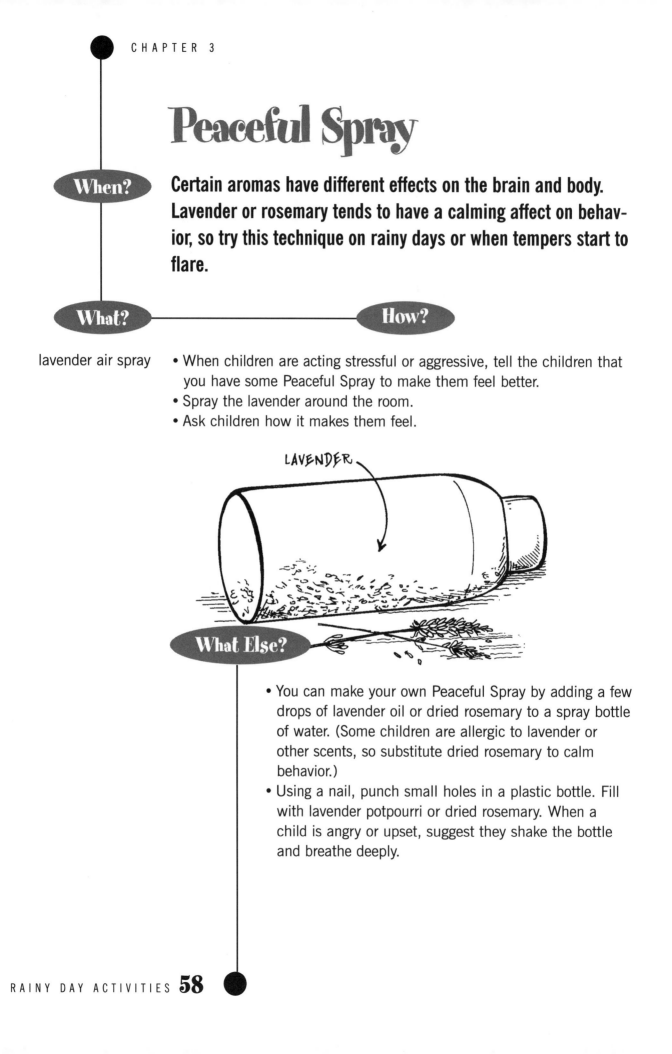

LAVENDER

What Else?

• You can make your own Peaceful Spray by adding a few drops of lavender oil or dried rosemary to a spray bottle of water. (Some children are allergic to lavender or other scents, so substitute dried rosemary to calm behavior.)
• Using a nail, punch small holes in a plastic bottle. Fill with lavender potpourri or dried rosemary. When a child is angry or upset, suggest they shake the bottle and breathe deeply.

Peace Talks

If children are fighting, this technique helps them express their thoughts and work towards mediation.

When?

What?

spiral notebook or large sheet of newsprint

crayons

pencils

How?

What else?

- Write "Peace Talks" on the notebook.
- If children are having an argument, ask them to sit at a table next to each other.
- Open up the book and say, "You draw what happened on this side" to the child on the right; and "You draw what happened here," to the child on the left.
- As children draw their versions of the incident they will begin to verbalize their thoughts.
- Many times they will resolve their own problems, or you may have to mediate by asking each child to discuss her picture and describe her point of view. Ask, "What do you think you can do about it?"

- Older children could write their explanation of what happened.
- Have children sit cross-legged on the floor, hold hands, and discuss what occurred. Eye contact and the sense of touch will often resolve conflicts.

Pick Me

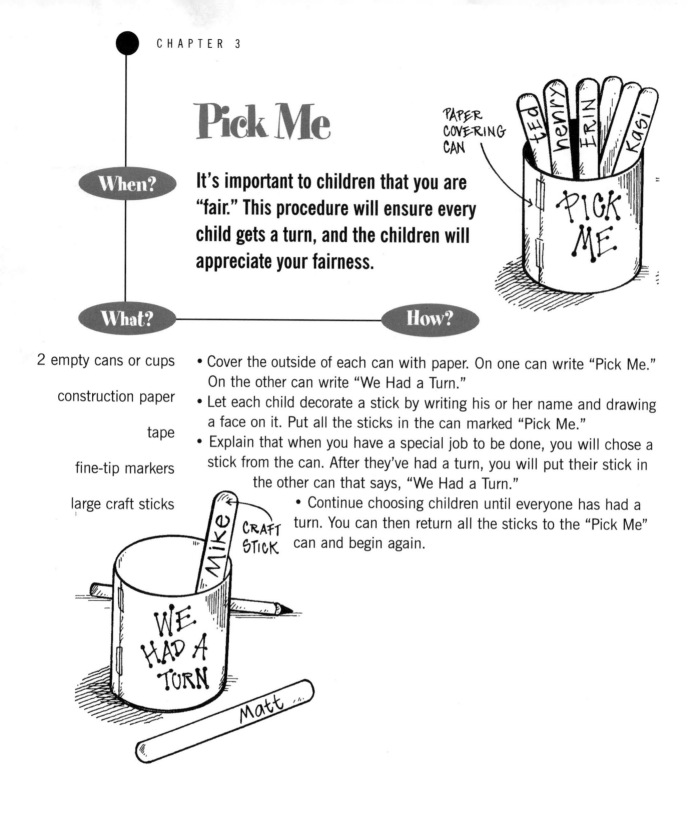

PAPER COVERING CAN

When? It's important to children that you are "fair." This procedure will ensure every child gets a turn, and the children will appreciate your fairness.

What?

How?

2 empty cans or cups

construction paper

tape

fine-tip markers

large craft sticks

- Cover the outside of each can with paper. On one can write "Pick Me." On the other can write "We Had a Turn."
- Let each child decorate a stick by writing his or her name and drawing a face on it. Put all the sticks in the can marked "Pick Me."
- Explain that when you have a special job to be done, you will chose a stick from the can. After they've had a turn, you will put their stick in the other can that says, "We Had a Turn."
- Continue choosing children until everyone has had a turn. You can then return all the sticks to the "Pick Me" can and begin again.

CRAFT STICK

Partner Picks

Use this idea to pair children randomly for games or other partner activities.

- You will need as many craft sticks as there are children in your classroom. Select two of each sticker and glue them to the bottom of each pair of sticks.
- Cover the can with construction paper and write "Partner Picks" on it. (Use extra stickers to decorate the can.)
- Place the craft sticks with the stickers down in the bottom in the can. Tell the children that when you pass around the can they should each choose a stick.
- When everyone has a stick, ask the children to get up and try to find the person with the sticker that matches theirs. That person will then be their partner for the specified activity.
- Listed below are a few projects that partners can enjoy:

Read a book together
Draw a picture or do an art project
Write together
Play in a learning center
Talk or solve a problem
Play a game
Work on a project

When?

What?

How?

large craft sticks

variety of stickers (in pairs)

can

glue

markers

What else?

construction paper

- Use seasonal stickers on craft sticks and vary through the year.
- For cooperative groups involving four children, cut old postcards or greeting cards into fourths. Pass out the pieces to the children and challenge them to find the matching pieces to make a puzzle. When they get the puzzle together, they'll have their cooperative group.

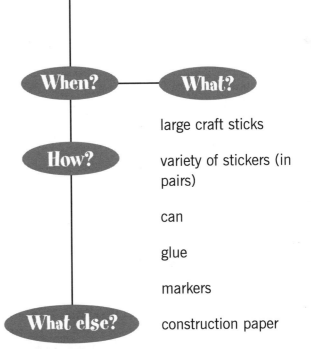

CAN COVERED WITH CONSTRUCTION PAPER

STICKS WITH STICKER (AT THE BOTTOM)

STICKERS

Partner Picks

STICKER

Cloud Ride

Take children for a Cloud Ride when it's time to relax.

When?

What?

How?

tape or CD of peaceful music

tape or CD player

- Begin playing the music.
- Ask the children to close their eyes.
- Lower your voice and talk slowly as you say the following.

We're going to take a cloud ride.
Hop on a white, fluffy cloud.
Here we go up in the blue sky.
Do you feel the wind in your face?
It's so peaceful up here.
Let your cloud take you to a place where you are happy.
Imagine where you are.
Think about who is with you.
You feel so good and peaceful.

What Else?

- Ask the children to imagine they are sitting on the beach in the sand listening to the waves break on the shore.
- Encourage the children to imagine riding on a magic carpet, sailing on a ship, or other imaginary adventures.
- Play tapes of environmental sounds, such as a rain forest, the ocean, the woods, and so on to relax the children.

Tighten-Relax

Tighten-Relax helps children learn about different parts of the body and release stress.

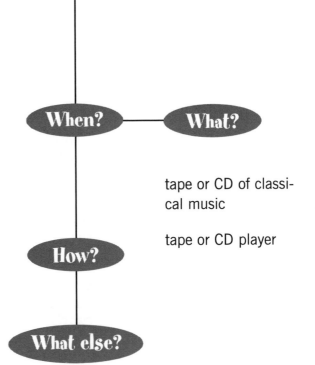

When?

What?

tape or CD of classical music

tape or CD player

How?

What else?

• Ask the children to lie on their backs with their eyes closed.
• Turn off the lights and play the music.
• With the children, work through the following exercise.

> Wiggle your toes. Tighten them up very tight.
> Tighter. Now let them relax.
> Wiggle your feet. Tighten them up very tight. Tighter.
> Now let them relax.
> Wiggle your legs…
> Wiggle your hands…
> Wiggle your arms…
> Wiggle your neck…
> Wiggle your head…
> Your whole body now feels warm and relaxed.

• Ask the children to stretch various parts of their bodies.
• Try this breathing exercise with children

> Pretend you are a balloon.
> Blow yourself up.
> Bigger, bigger!
> Now slowly let out all of the air.
> Put your hands on your tummy.
> Now blow it up with air.
> Do you feel it getting bigger and bigger?
> Now slowly let out all the air.

INDEX